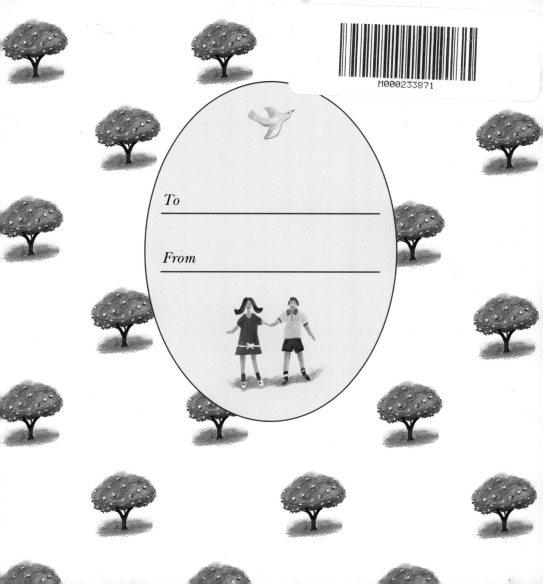

To _____

From _____

Acknowledgments
Bible extracts (introduction) from Exodus 20:22–23, Deuteronomy 6:4–7, Psalm 1 (adapted). The Ten Commandments adapted from Exodus 20:1–17, Deuteronomy 5:7–21. Scriptures quoted from the Good News Bible published by The Bible Societies/HarperCollins Publishers Ltd, UK © American Bible Society 1966, 1971, 1976, 1992, used with permission.

Text copyright © 2000 Lois Rock.
Illustrations copyright © 2000 Debbie Lush.

Original edition published in English under the title **The Ten Commandments** by Lion Publishing plc, Oxford, England.

Copyright © Lion Publishing plc 2000

ISBN: 0-8091-6691-7

Published in the United States and Canada by Paulist Press
997 Macarthur Boulevard
Mahwah, New Jersey 07430

www.paulistpress.com

Printed and bound in Singapore

The *10* Commandments

Words of wisdom from the Bible

Retold by Lois Rock
Illustrated by Debbie Lush

PAULIST PRESS
New York/Mahwah, New Jersey

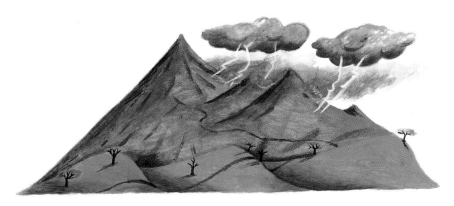

ABOUT THE TEN COMMANDMENTS

*L**ong ago, as the Bible says, a man named Moses went to the top of a holy mountain named Sinai. There, on a rocky peak that rises above the barren land to the east of Egypt, God gave him the commandments that were to guide his people.*

On the plain below, the people of Israel watched in fear. Thunder crashed, and a mighty trumpet blast echoed among the rocks. Lightning flashed down from the summit; smoke billowed around the mountainside.

Moses returned with a message from God: "You have seen how I, the Lord, have spoken to you from heaven. Do not make for yourselves gods of silver or gold to be worshiped in addition to me."

It was tempting to do so, nonetheless. The nations all around made images of wood, stone and metal, and worshiped them as gods. Some of these nations had grown powerful and wealthy. The Israelites were a refugee nation, on the run from the land of Egypt, where they had been slaves. So they did as other powerful nations had done and built a golden calf to worship.

Moses was stern in his response. He reminded his people that God had enabled them to escape, making for them a pathway through the sea. God had provided them with food and water in the wilderness. Now God was taking them to a land that they could make their home, and where they would be free to live as God's people. The laws told them how to worship God, and how to treat their fellow human beings with justice, honesty and goodness. By keeping God's laws, they would enjoy the fullness of God's blessing in their new land.

"Israel, remember this! The Lord–and the Lord alone–is our God. Love the Lord your God with all your heart, with all your soul, and with all your strength. Never forget these commands that I am giving you today. Teach them to your children. Repeat them when you are at home and when you are away, when you are resting and when you are working."

The commandments were written on tablets of stone and kept in a golden box in the innermost part of the nation's place of worship. They were recorded in the writings of the people and copied faithfully from scroll to scroll. They were handed down from generation to generation, and poets sang of the greatness of the law.

"Happy are those who find joy in obeying the law of the Lord.
They are like trees that grow beside a stream,
That bear fruit at the right time,
And whose leaves do not dry up.
The righteous are guided and protected by the Lord."

The Ten Commandments are the great summary of all the laws.
They belong to and are cherished by the descendants of the people
of Israel, known today as the Jews, and they are honored by
Christians, who share the same heritage of stories. They are respected
all over the world for the guidance they give in showing people a way
to live that is good and right.

God spoke all these words, saying,

I am the Lord your God, who brought you out of the land of Egypt...
You shall have no other gods but me.

If you would keep these commandments, then you must know that there is one God, one alone whom you must honor.

You shall not make for yourself graven images…you shall not bow down to them or serve them.

Beware of worshiping material things.
Do not put your trust in them.

You shall not take the name
of the Lord your God in vain.

Be careful when you speak of God.
Do not claim that you can speak
on God's behalf.

Remember the sabbath day and keep it holy.

Enjoy the rhythm of the days:

six for work

and one for rest.

Honor your father
and your mother.

*Give respect to those
who gave birth to you,
those who raised you.*

You shall not kill.

*God alone gives life,
and you do not have the
right to take it away.*

You shall not
commit adultery.

God made man and woman to live together in faithfulness and love all their lives.

You shall
not steal.

*Respect what
belongs to others...
it is theirs to enjoy.*

You shall not bear false witness against your neighbor.

Speak the truth of others; weave no lies.

You shall not covet anything
that is your neighbor's.

*Do not look greedily at what
others have. Only trust in God,
and do good.*